She's In Hiding

Dr. Clarence E S Jones DD

Dedication

To the **Bronx Pentecostal Deliverance Center**, the sacred home where my faith has been nurtured, my spirit strengthened, and my heart set free. Your prayers have been a fortress in my journey, and your love has been the wind beneath these pages.

To the **ministers and members of the International House of Praise**, whose unwavering support and steadfast faith have been a beacon of light during my darkest nights. Your belief in God's redemptive power continues to inspire me to carry His message with every word I write.

To **Bishop M.K. Baxter** and the **Cathedral of Love Church** for your mentorship, wisdom, and unwavering belief in the power of God's love and restoration. You have been a guiding light, showing me how to live out faith with courage and compassion. I thank God for your leadership and the legacy of love you continue to build.

To **Dr. Josette Rey**, my wonderful mother-in-law, whose love, wisdom, and unwavering faith have been a source of strength and encouragement. Your kindness reflects the heart of Christ, and your support has meant the world to me.

To **Apostle Joseline Rey-Sutton**, a powerhouse of faith and a vessel of God's anointing. Your prayers, guidance, and unwavering belief in God's purpose for my life have been a foundation upon which I've learned. Your impact is immeasurable, and your legacy shines brightly for all to see.

To my beloved wife, **Josy Rey-Jones**, my high school sweetheart, my sunshine on a cloudy day, the melody in my life's song. You are the embodiment of God's grace and love, a reminder of His promise of joy, steadfastness, and enduring partnership. Without you, I am but a shadow; with you, I am complete.

To my wonderful daughter, Evangelist **Latoya T. Jones Herbert**, my firstborn and the pride of my heart. You reflect God's glory in your strength and kindness. Watching you grow has been one of my greatest blessings, and I am endlessly proud of the woman you've become.

To my second and beautiful daughter, **Chrisianna Renee Jones**, a radiant light in this world. Your joy, resilience, and faithfulness are a testament to God's abundant blessings. You are a treasure, a living testimony of His love in my life.

To my awesome son, my "replacement," **Curtis Emmanuel Jones**, my pride and legacy. You are proof of God's goodness, a young man filled with strength, integrity, and purpose. Watching you rise into the person God created you to be fills my heart with joy.

This book is for you, my loved ones, and anyone who has sought refuge in the shadow of God's wings. May these pages speak of His healing, His mercy, and His unending love.

In the Master service, Dr Clarence E. S. Jones 'DD

Acknowledgment

To my sunshine on the cloudy day, my beloved wife and high school sweetheart, Pastor Josy Jones: your unwavering love, wisdom, and faith have been my anchor and my inspiration. You are not only my partner in ministry but also a living example of God's grace and strength. You have stood by me with unshakable faith, encouraging me to pursue the vision God has placed in my heart. Thank you for being my prayer warrior, my confidant, and my greatest supporter. Your love is a reflection of God's unending care, and your steadfastness has made this journey possible. I am endlessly grateful to you, not only for your role in this work but for the gift of you in my life. Truly, you are my sunshine when the days grow dark, a reminder of God's goodness.

To my three beautiful children, Curtis, Latoya, and Chrisianna Jones: you are my pride, my joy, and my legacy. Each of you brings a unique light to my life, shining brightly with the gifts God has given you. Curtis, your strength and determination inspire me. Latoya, your compassion and wisdom remind me of God's gentleness. Chrisianna, your boundless energy, and creativity fill my heart with joy. Thank you for your patience, your prayers, and your unwavering belief in me as I worked on this project. Your laughter has been a balm to my soul, and your love is a source of constant motivation. You remind me daily of the incredible blessings that God has entrusted to me as your father.

And to the wonderful members of my spiritual family from The International House of Praise church, my spiritual sons and daughters into whom I pour and who also pour into me. I realized that you have become a part of my inspiration being able to plant this resource and ministry tool to the healing of many men and women across the world. Sending them a message from God that we would no longer live in the dark realm hidden from society, but our God will open us up into his marvelous light a real light in a dark world.

This book is as much a tribute to my family as it is a work of ministry. To my wife and children, your love has been the guiding light in my life, the foundation upon which I stand, and the inspiration that has carried me through the challenges of this journey. I dedicate this acknowledgment to the immeasurable impact you have made on my heart and my calling. I love you more deeply than words can ever express, and I thank God every day for the gift of you in my life.

Contents

Preface

In a world where silence often conceals the most profound wounds, *She's in Hiding* emerges as a poignant and necessary voice, calling us out of the shadows and into the healing light of God's love. This book is not just a collection of stories; it is a testament to the resilience of the human spirit and the transformative power of faith.

Through the lives of Sarah, Emma, and Tasha, we are invited into an intimate exploration of pain, perseverance, and redemption. These women represent so many who have been silenced by abuse, shame, and fear. Yet, through their journeys, we see the undeniable truth that no wound is too deep, no scar too permanent, for the healing touch of the Savior.

As a minister and counselor, I have walked alongside countless individuals who, like the women in this book, have endured unspeakable pain. I have seen firsthand how God's grace can turn mourning into dancing, despair into hope, and brokenness into beauty. The stories within these pages serve as a powerful reminder that our God is a God of restoration who delights in making all things new.

She's in Hiding also serves as a clarion call to those who may still be hiding in their pain. It challenges us to step out of the darkness and into the embrace of a loving community and a compassionate Creator. For those who feel unseen, unheard, or unworthy, this book offers an unwavering message: God sees you, He hears you, and He calls you by name.

The inclusion of Scripture throughout the narrative not only grounds these stories in God's truth but also provides a lifeline for readers who may be navigating their own paths to healing.

To the reader, I encourage you to approach this book with an open heart. Whether you see yourself in Sarah's journey of rediscovering confidence, Emma's story of finding her voice, or Tasha's transformation into a beacon of hope, may you be reminded that God's love knows no bounds. And if you have yet to experience His healing, may this book inspire you to take that first courageous step.

May *She's in Hiding* be a source of strength, encouragement, and renewal for all who read it. And may it serve as a reminder that, in Christ, we are never truly hidden—we are seen, known, and deeply loved.

In His Service,

Dr. Clarence E S Jones, DD

Introduction

There are moments in life when pain and adversity seem to have the final word when the trials we face threaten to bury us under the weight of despair. Yet, as believers, we know that our God is a God of redemption who brings beauty from ashes and turns mourning into dancing. It is with this conviction that I present to you *She's in Hiding*.

This book is more than a collection of stories; it is a ministry to the brokenhearted, a lifeline for those who feel unseen, and a declaration of hope for anyone who has ever felt trapped by their circumstances. Through the lives of Sarah, Emma, and Tasha, you will witness the transformative power of faith in action. Each of these women faced unimaginable struggles—physical, emotional, and spiritual—but through God's grace, they found healing, purpose, and a renewed sense of identity.

Why is this book important? Because there are countless women, and indeed men, who are still hiding—hiding from their pain, their past, and sometimes even from God. They have built walls around their hearts, convinced that their scars disqualify them from the abundant life Christ promises. *She's in Hiding* and is here to shatter those walls. It is a reminder that God sees you, He loves you, and He has a plan for your life—a plan to give you hope and a future (Jeremiah 29:11).

As you read these pages, you will find not only stories of pain but also stories of triumph. You will see how Scripture serves as a guiding light, leading these women out of the shadows and into the fullness of God's grace. You will witness the beauty of community and the power of sharing your story. Most importantly, you will be reminded that your past does not define you—God does.

To anyone who has ever felt like they are in hiding, this book is for you. It is my prayer that these stories will inspire you to step out of the darkness and into the marvelous light of God's love. It is time to stop hiding. It is time to live boldly, courageously, and purposefully, knowing that God's plans for you are good.

As you journey through this book, may you feel the presence of the Holy Spirit guiding you, comforting you, and strengthening you. May you be reminded that even in your darkest moments, God is working all things together for your good (Romans 8:28). And may you come away with a renewed sense of hope, ready to embrace the destiny that God has prepared for you.

In His Service,

Dr. Clarence E S Jones, DD

PART 1
SARAH'S STORY

Chapter One
Sarah's Story

Sarah sat on the edge of her bed, staring at the suitcase that had been packed and unpacked more times than she could count. The bruises on her arms, fading from purple to yellow, told the story of her last attempt to leave. He had caught her as she reached for the door, his grip ironclad, his words venomous.

"You think you can leave me?" he'd spat, slamming her against the wall. "You're nothing without me."

For eight years, she'd endured his wrath. The fists, the insults, the nights spent crying on the bathroom floor while he slept soundly in their bed. Every time she thought about leaving, his voice echoed in her mind: *You're weak. No one else will ever want you.* And she believed him. The vibrant, confident lawyer she once was had disappeared, replaced by a shadow of a woman too afraid to speak, to fight, to hope.

But it wasn't just the physical pain that broke her. It was the isolation. The way he'd cut her off from friends and family, convincing her they didn't care, that they wouldn't believe her even if she told them. It was the little things—the way he'd criticize her cooking, her clothes, the way she walked or laughed.

She's In Hiding

"You're embarrassing," he'd say, sneering. And she'd shrink a little more each time.

She remembered one night vividly, the night she thought she might die. He'd come home drunk, anger radiating off him like heat. She'd accidentally left a light on in the kitchen. That was all it took. His hand lashed out before she could explain, sending her sprawling onto the cold tile floor.

"Can't you do anything right?" he'd bellowed. She'd stayed there for hours after he stormed off, too afraid to move.

And yet, here she was. Still alive. Still breathing. And now, for the first time in years, she felt something stir within her—a flicker of defiance, of hope.

It started when she found her grandmother's Bible. She'd been cleaning out a closet, sorting through boxes of memories she hadn't touched since her wedding day. There it was, tucked away beneath a pile of old sweaters. The cover was worn, the pages yellowed, but as she opened it, the words seemed to leap off the page: *The Lord is my light and my salvation—whom shall I fear? The Lord is the stronghold of my life—of whom shall I be afraid?* (Psalm 27:1).

Tears blurred her vision as she read. She'd grown up in church, memorizing verses like this one, but she'd long since stopped believing they applied to her. Yet, in that moment, she felt something she hadn't felt in years: courage.

Sarah began reading the Psalms every day, clinging to the promises of protection and deliverance like a lifeline. Slowly, she felt the chains of fear begin to loosen. She started taking small steps—reaching out to an old friend, visiting a church service, sitting in the back where she could slip out unnoticed.

One Sunday, the pastor's message hit her like a bolt of lightning. He spoke about the woman with the issue of blood, how she'd reached out in desperation to touch Jesus' robe.

"Sometimes," he said, "you have to fight through the crowd, through the fear, through the lies the enemy whispers in your ear, and just reach out. Jesus is waiting for you."

That was the moment Sarah decided to stop hiding. She approached the pastor after the service, her hands trembling as she introduced herself. He listened patiently as she shared her story, his eyes filled with compassion.

"You're not alone," he told her. "God has a plan for you, Sarah. He's not done with you yet."

The pastor connected her with a counselor, and for the first time, Sarah began to unpack the years of pain she'd buried deep inside. She learned to pray again, not the timid, half-hearted prayers of her past, but bold, fervent cries for healing and strength. She joined a women's Bible study, finding comfort and camaraderie among others who had walked similar paths.

Week by week, Sarah felt herself growing stronger. She started volunteering at a local shelter for abuse survivors, using her legal skills to help women navigate restraining orders and custody battles. It was there that she realized her pain had a purpose.

"If I can make it out," she told one woman, "you can too. God hasn't forgotten you."

The turning point came not just for Sarah but for her husband, Mark. After Sarah finally left, taking refuge at the shelter, Mark was forced to confront his actions. At first, he was enraged, blaming her for leaving and accusing her of ruining their family. But as the weeks passed, the silence in their home became deafening. For the first time, he felt the weight of his own emptiness.

One night, in a moment of despair, Mark stumbled across one of Sarah's forgotten Bibles. It lay on the nightstand, open to a passage she had highlighted years before: *"Create in me a clean heart, O God, and renew a right spirit within me."* (Psalm 51:10). The words pierced his heart. He fell to his knees, sobbing, as the reality of his actions came crashing down.

Mark sought out the same pastor Sarah had confided in. Through tears, he confessed his sins and the pain he had inflicted on his wife. The pastor listened, then prayed with him, urging him to seek God's forgiveness and begin the long journey of change.

Mark joined a men's accountability group at the church, where he met other men who had struggled with anger and control. Slowly, he began to transform. He attended counseling sessions, delved into the root of his rage, and started reading the Bible daily. Over time, his hardened heart softened.

When Mark and Sarah eventually crossed paths again, it was at a church service. Sarah was hesitant, her guard still up, but she saw the change in him—the humility, the genuine remorse. He apologized, not with empty words but with a broken spirit, acknowledging the depth of his wrongs and the pain he had caused.

God himself begins to work on the reconciliation between the two Hearts that have been broken. Knowing that God is a mender of broken pieces, he began putting the pieces back together again, redeeming their ministries and their lives to him, and again becoming the third chord in their marriage and strengthening their bond greater than they ever have been before, whom God put together let no man put asunder.

That night, Sarah and her husband realized they had been called to more than just survival. They had been called to the Ministry. Today, she travels the world as an evangelist, sharing her story with women from all walks of life. Her message is simple but powerful: "If God can bring me out, He can do the same for you. Don't hide. Step into the light. Your healing begins when you let Him in."

As she closes every sermon, she reminds her audience of Isaiah 41:10: *"So do not fear, for I am with you; do not be dismayed, for I am your God. I will strengthen you and help you; I will uphold you with my righteous right hand."*

Chapter Two
A New Mission

The courthouse smelled the same—an unchanging mix of paper, coffee, and determination. Sarah's heels clicked softly against the polished floors as she walked through the halls she once knew so well. Every step was a mix of nostalgia and trepidation, but the fear didn't dominate her this time.

Her first stop was Judge Holden's office, where she'd spent hours litigating high-profile cases. Now, standing at the doorway, she hesitated before knocking.

"Come in," a familiar voice called.

Sarah pushed the door open, her breath catching as the judge's piercing blue eyes met hers.

"Sarah?" Judge Holden leaned forward, his surprise evident. "I can't believe it. How have you been?"

"It's been… a journey," she said, offering a tentative smile.

"I heard you left the firm. I didn't think I'd see you back here."

Sarah straightened her posture. "I'm not here to litigate, Your Honor. I want to start a legal aid initiative for survivors of domestic abuse—pro bono representation, counseling referrals, the works. I know how hard it is for women to escape those situations, and I want to help."

The judge studied her for a long moment before nodding. "That's ambitious, Sarah. But if anyone can do it, it's you."

Hearing those words felt like the first rays of sunlight breaking through the clouds.

***

Sarah threw herself into the project with a passion she hadn't felt in years. She reached out to former colleagues, nonprofits, and local churches, forming a network of resources. Grace Fellowship Church became a cornerstone of the initiative, offering space for meetings and workshops.

One of her first clients was a young woman named Elena, barely in her twenties, with a toddler clinging to her side. Her story mirrored Sarah's in so many painful ways—years of manipulation, fear, and feeling trapped.

"Elena," Sarah said during their first meeting, "you're not alone in this. I've been where you are, and I promise you, there's a way out."

The words felt heavy yet freeing. Sarah had avoided her past for so long, afraid of its power over her. Now, she was using it to help others find hope.

***

Despite the progress, Sarah's journey wasn't without setbacks. There were nights when the memories crept back, unbidden and sharp. On one such night, she found herself staring at her grandmother's Bible, her fingers tracing the worn cover.

She opened to a passage she had marked weeks ago: Isaiah 41:10. "Do not fear, for I am with you; do not be dismayed, for I am your God. I will strengthen you and help you; I will uphold you with my righteous right hand."

As the words sank in, Sarah closed her eyes and prayed. "Lord, I can't do this without You. Give me the strength to keep going."

The next morning, she woke with a renewed sense of purpose.

***

Months later, the courtroom was packed for one of Sarah's cases. Elena was seeking a restraining order against her abusive ex-partner, and Sarah stood by her side, armed with evidence and a quiet resolve.

As she delivered her closing argument, Sarah's voice was steady and firm. "Your Honor, my client is not just asking for protection—she's asking for a chance to rebuild her life, free from fear and harm. I urge the court to grant her that chance."

When the judge ruled in their favor, Elena burst into tears, clutching Sarah's hand.

"Thank you," she whispered.

As Sarah walked out of the courthouse that day, she realized something profound: helping others heal was healing her, too.

***

One evening, during a Bible study session, Pastor Greg approached Sarah.

"You've come a long way," he said, his voice filled with warmth.

Sarah nodded, smiling. "I couldn't have done it without God—or this church."

Pastor Greg looked thoughtful. "You know, Sarah, your story could inspire others. Have you thought about sharing it?"

The idea terrified her but also sparked something inside—a desire to use her voice, not just her skills, to make a difference.

"I'll think about it," she said.

And for the first time in years, Sarah felt ready to face whatever came next.

Chapter Three
The Courage to Speak

Sarah sat at her desk, staring at the invitation on her laptop screen.

"Women's Renewal Conference: Stories of Faith and Resilience."

The church organizing the event had reached out to her after hearing about her legal aid initiative. They wanted her to share her testimony—a deeply personal recounting of her journey from abuse to faith.

Her initial reaction was to decline. The thought of standing in front of hundreds of strangers, exposing the rawest parts of her life, made her stomach churn. But the words of Pastor Greg echoed in her mind: *"Your story could inspire others."*

She hesitated, then typed a single word in response: *Yes.*

***

The day of the conference arrived faster than Sarah anticipated. Dressed in a simple navy dress, she clutched her grandmother's Bible tightly as she waited backstage. The room buzzed with chatter and anticipation, the audience far larger than she had imagined.

"Are you ready?" a volunteer asked, peeking her head through the curtain.

Sarah took a deep breath. "As ready as I'll ever be."

As she stepped onto the stage, the lights blinded her momentarily. The applause was warm but overwhelming. She approached the microphone, her hands trembling.

"Good afternoon," she began, her voice shaky. "My name is Sarah, and I'd like to share a story about hiding—and finding hope."

***

She started at the beginning: the whirlwind romance, the subtle signs of control, and the years of fear that followed. The words came haltingly at first, but as she spoke, the weight of her story seemed to lift.

"I thought I was alone," she said, scanning the faces in the crowd.

"I believed no one could understand what I was going through. But then I found this."

She held up her grandmother's Bible. "And in these pages, I found strength I didn't know I had. I found a God who saw me, even in my darkest moments."

She spoke about the verses that had carried her through, the community at Grace Fellowship that had embraced her, and the legal aid initiative that had become her mission.

"Today, I stand here not as a victim but as a survivor," she said, her voice steady.

"And I want you to know that healing is possible. You don't have to hide anymore."

The room was silent for a moment, then erupted in applause.

***

After the session, women approached her, some with tears in their eyes. They shared their own stories—of pain, resilience, and hope. One woman handed her a note: *"Thank you for reminding me that I'm not alone."*

That evening, as Sarah sat in her hotel room, she opened her Bible to Psalm 23. She read the familiar words aloud: "Even though I walk through the darkest valley, I will fear no evil, for You are with me."

She felt a sense of peace for the first time—not because the journey was over, but because she was no longer walking it alone.

***

She's In Hiding

The conference marked a turning point for Sarah. Invitations to speak at other events followed, and she shared her story with a little more confidence each time.

Her work at the legal aid initiative flourished, with more volunteers and donations pouring in. Grace Fellowship Church expanded its outreach programs, offering workshops on faith-based healing and empowerment.

Through it all, Sarah remained grounded in her faith, knowing that a greater purpose guided every step she took.

One Sunday, after a particularly moving service, Pastor Greg approached her with a knowing smile.

"I think you've found your calling, Sarah," he said.

She smiled back. "I think so too."

Chapter Four

A New Calling

The sanctuary of Grace Fellowship Church was packed. Women from all walks of life filled the pews, their faces reflecting a mixture of anticipation and hope. Sarah stood in the front, flanked by Pastor Greg and the elders, her heart pounding as they prayed over her.

"Today," Pastor Greg announced, his voice resonating with conviction, "we appoint Sarah Mitchell to the ministry of evangelism. She has been called to spread the message of hope, healing, and the power of God's love to women around the world."

The congregation erupted in applause, but Sarah barely heard it. Her mind was on the journey that had brought her to this moment—every tear, every prayer, every small step toward healing. She felt a deep sense of gratitude and awe that God had turned her pain into purpose.

As Pastor Greg handed her the microphone, Sarah took a deep breath and stepped forward.

"Thank you," she began, her voice steady. "This moment is not just about me. It's about the God who saw me when I was broken, hiding, and hopeless. It's about the women—like so many of you—who feel unseen and unheard."

She paused, looking out over the crowd. "There was a time when I believed the darkness would consume me. But God met me there. He didn't just pull me out of the shadows—He walked with me through them. And now, He's given me the privilege of walking with others."

Sarah shared a condensed version of her story, focusing on the moments when God's presence had been most evident. She spoke of the Bible verses that had strengthened her, the community that had embraced her, and the calling that had grown in her heart.

"God can take what was meant for harm and use it for good," she said, her voice rising with passion. "He can turn your pain into purpose, your fear into faith, your brokenness into beauty. Whatever you've been through—whether it's abuse, betrayal, or loss—God is able to bring you out of it."

She scanned the room, meeting the eyes of women who nodded, cried, and held onto her every word.

"You are not forgotten," she continued. "You are loved. And there is nothing so broken that God cannot restore it."

The altar call that followed was powerful. Women came forward, many of them weeping, as they sought prayer and rededication to their faith. Sarah prayed with them, feeling the weight and privilege of her new role.

***

Over the next year, Sarah's ministry grew rapidly. She traveled across the country and eventually the world, sharing her testimony at conferences, retreats, and women's shelters. She partnered with churches and organizations, combining her legal background with her ministry to provide holistic support for abuse survivors.

Her message was always the same: *"God sees you. He loves you. And He can bring you out of the darkness."*

Through every speech, every prayer, and every conversation, Sarah saw lives transformed—not because of her, but because of the God who had transformed her own life.

***

One evening, as she prepared for another speaking engagement, Sarah opened her Bible to Isaiah 61:1:

"The Spirit of the Lord God is upon me, because the Lord has anointed me to bring good news to the afflicted; He has sent me to bind up the brokenhearted, to proclaim liberty to captives and freedom to prisoners."

Tears filled her eyes as she whispered, "Thank You, Lord, for using me."

She's In Hiding

Her journey had come full circle. The woman who had once been hiding was now a beacon of light for others, proof that healing and hope were possible through faith.

And as long as there were women who needed to hear that message, Sarah would continue to share it.

Epilogue

For those reading Sarah's story who have experienced pain, fear, or brokenness, know this: God is able. He sees your tears, hears your prayers, and walks with you, even in the darkest valleys. There is hope, there is healing, and there is a future beyond what you can imagine.

You are not alone.

PART 2

EMMA'S STORY

Chapter Five
Wilted Roots

The garden was Emma's sanctuary. It was the only place where she felt safe, the only space where she could control what grew and what didn't. Rows of roses, daisies, and marigolds flourished under her care, their bright colors starkly contrasting with the darkness she carried inside.

At 42, Emma's world was small—deliberately so. The outside world had only brought pain: a childhood scarred by her father's cruelty, followed by a marriage that mirrored the same abuse. The words they had spoken to her over the years still echoed in her mind: "You're useless. You'll never be good enough."

She believed them.

So Emma stayed home, hiding behind the safety of her garden. She rarely went beyond her gate except for necessities. The idea of interacting with others was too overwhelming; her shame and fear kept her isolated.

One afternoon, as she trimmed her roses, a voice interrupted her thoughts.

"Beautiful garden."

She's In Hiding

Emma looked up, startled. Her neighbor, Mrs. Willis, was holding a basket of fresh vegetables. She was a kind woman in her 60s, known for her warm smile and gentle demeanor.

"Thank you," Emma replied quietly, hoping the conversation would end there.

But Mrs. Willis didn't leave. "We're having a women's group at church this Thursday. It's just a few of us getting together to talk and pray. You should come."

Emma froze. "I don't think so," she said, avoiding eye contact.

Mrs. Willis didn't push. She simply smiled. "If you change your mind, we'd love to have you. You're always welcome."

As she walked away, Emma felt a twinge of curiosity—something she hadn't felt in years.

***

The next Thursday, Emma found herself pacing in her living room, the church flyer in her hand. She told herself she wasn't going, but something inside her wouldn't let the idea go.

Finally, she grabbed her coat and stepped out of the house.

***

The women's group met in a small room at Grace Fellowship Church. As Emma entered, her heart raced. She almost turned back, but Mrs. Willis spotted her and waved her over.

"We're so glad you came," she said, guiding Emma to a seat.

The meeting began with introductions and prayer. As the women shared their struggles and victories, Emma was struck by their openness. They spoke of hardships—divorce, illness, loss— with a raw honesty that both intimidated and inspired her.

When it was Emma's turn to speak, she hesitated. "I... I don't really know what to say," she admitted, her voice barely above a whisper.

"That's okay," Mrs. Willis said gently. "You're here, and that's enough."

For the first time in years, Emma felt a spark of hope.

***

That night, Emma began journaling. At first, it was just scattered thoughts—questions to God, fragments of memories. But over time, her journal became a place of prayer, a space where she poured out her pain and fears.

One entry read: *"Lord, I don't know if You can fix someone like me. But if You're there, please help me."*

***

She's In Hiding

As weeks turned into months, Emma continued attending the women's group. She began to see that she wasn't alone in her struggles, and the shame that had weighed her down started to lift.

One evening, the group discussed forgiveness.

"Forgiveness doesn't mean excusing what they did," Mrs. Willis said.

"It means releasing their hold over you. It's for your freedom, not theirs."

The words hit Emma like a bolt of lightning. She realized she had been carrying the weight of her past for too long.

That night, she wrote in her journal: *"I forgive them—not because they deserve it, but because I deserve peace."*

It wasn't easy. Forgiveness came slowly, one painful memory at a time. But with each step, Emma felt lighter, freer.

***

Emma's garden began to take on new meaning. She started planting new flowers, symbolizing her growth and renewal. The once-wilted roses bloomed brighter than ever, mirroring the change within her.

One Sunday, after a church service, Mrs. Willis approached her.

"You've come such a long way, Emma," she said. "Have you ever thought about mentoring young women? Sharing your story could help so many."

The idea terrified Emma but also sparked something inside her—a desire to give back, to use her pain for a purpose.

***

Months later, Emma led her first mentoring session at church. She shared her journey with a small group of young women, many of whom were struggling with their own scars.

"You are not what happened to you," she told them, her voice steady. "You are loved, and you are enough. God can take the broken pieces of your life and make something beautiful."

As the session ended, one of the girls hugged Emma tightly. "Thank you," she said, tears in her eyes. "I needed to hear that."

Emma smiled, feeling a sense of joy she hadn't known in years.

Her garden was no longer her hiding place. It was a place of growth, healing, and hope—a reflection of the woman she was becoming.

And she knew her journey was just beginning.

Chapter Six

A Voice in the Wilderness

Emma stood at the pulpit, her once-quiet demeanor replaced with a presence that commanded attention. The sanctuary was filled with women of all ages—some curious, some desperate for hope, others just needing to feel seen. Emma's voice, soft yet resolute, carried through the room.

"I used to believe I had no voice," she began, her eyes scanning the audience.

"For years, I let fear and shame keep me silent. But I'm here to tell you, God didn't create us to live in the shadows. He created us to live in His light."

She paused, opening her Bible to Jeremiah 29:11. "The Lord says, *'For I know the plans I have for you,' declares the Lord, 'plans to prosper you and not to harm you, plans to give you hope and a future.'*"

Her voice grew stronger as she continued. "If you've been told you're worthless, that your life doesn't matter, I want you to know those are lies. God has a plan for you—a destiny that no one can take away."

***

Emma's journey to becoming a powerful voice in the kingdom of God had been unexpected but undeniable. It started with her mentoring sessions, where she found immense fulfillment in guiding young women through their struggles. As word of her work spread, Emma was invited to speak at women's conferences, churches, and shelters.

Her message was simple yet profound: *"If I can change your mind, you can change your destiny."*

Emma often shared the verse from 2 Timothy 1:7: *"For God has not given us a spirit of fear, but of power and of love and of a sound mind."* She used it to remind women that they had the power to break free from fear and reclaim their lives.

***

One evening, Emma visited a women's shelter in a nearby city. The room was filled with women who had endured unimaginable pain. Many of them avoided eye contact, and their postures slumped in defeat. Emma recognized herself in their brokenness, and it fueled her determination.

"I know what it's like to feel powerless," she began. "To believe the lies that tell you you'll never be free. But I'm standing here today as proof that those lies don't define you."

She shared her story, weaving in scriptures that had carried her through her darkest moments. She ended with Isaiah 61:3: *"To bestow on them a crown of beauty instead of ashes, the oil of joy instead of mourning, and a garment of praise instead of a spirit of despair."*

As she spoke, the women began to lift their heads, their eyes meeting hers. By the end of the session, tears were flowing, and hope had sparked in hearts that had long been hardened.

***

Emma's ministry grew not because of her eloquence but because of her authenticity. She didn't shy away from her past; instead, she used it to demonstrate God's power to redeem and restore.

One of her favorite events was hosting workshops called "Reclaiming Your Voice," where she taught women how to pray boldly, speak truth over their lives, and take steps toward healing.

During one such workshop, a young woman named Tasha approached her.

"Ms. Emma," Tasha said hesitantly, "how did you forgive them? The people who hurt you?"

Emma smiled gently. "It wasn't easy, Tasha. But I realized that forgiveness wasn't for them—it was for me. It was my way of saying, 'You don't control me anymore.' And I could only do it through God's strength."

Tasha nodded, tears streaming down her face. "I want that freedom, too."

Emma took her hands and prayed with her, feeling the Holy Spirit move in the room.

***

Years later, Emma stood on a stage in front of thousands at a women's conference. Her once-small voice now echoed across stadiums, her message reaching women around the world.

"God doesn't call the perfect," she said, her voice steady with conviction. "He calls the willing. And if you're willing to trust Him, He'll take the broken pieces of your life and create something beautiful."

She looked into the crowd, meeting the eyes of women who had traveled from near and far to hear her speak. "I don't know your story, but I know this: God does. And He's not finished with you. Your voice matters. Your life matters. If you let Him, He will use you in ways you can't even imagine."

Emma ended with her favorite verse, Ephesians 3:20: *"Now to Him who is able to do immeasurably more than all we ask or imagine, according to His power that is at work within us."*

The applause was thunderous, but Emma's focus wasn't on the noise. It was on the women whose lives were being transformed—not because of her, but because of the God she served.

***

Emma felt a deep sense of fulfillment as she walked off the stage. She was no longer the woman who hid in her garden, afraid of the world. She was a force to be reckoned with—a voice in the kingdom of God, proclaiming His love and power to anyone who would listen.

And she knew that for every woman who found her voice, another life would be changed.

***

Chapter Seven
Tasha's New Beginning

The fluorescent lights of the diner flickered faintly, casting a dull glow over the late-night crowd. Tasha moved through the aisles with practiced efficiency, her smile barely masking the emptiness she felt inside. At just 25 years old, she had already lived through more pain than most people could imagine. Years in foster care had taught her not to trust anyone—not the adults who broke promises, nor the system that failed her. She was alone in every sense of the word.

It was just another long, quiet night until she noticed the elderly woman at table four. A regular customer, the woman always left a kind word or compliment along with her payment. But tonight, there was something different. When Tasha cleared the table, she found a small folded note tucked under the plate.

She opened it hesitantly, expecting a simple thank-you. Instead, the note read: *"You are fearfully and wonderfully made."* *—Psalm 139:14.*

The words stopped her in her tracks. *Me? Fearfully and wonderfully made?* It was a concept so foreign to her that it felt like a language she didn't understand. Her mind drifted back to the darkest days of her life, the ones she tried so hard to forget.

The Wounds of the Past

Tasha's time in foster care was a patchwork of instability and heartache. One home blurred into the next, each filled with unspoken rules and broken promises. At twelve, her world darkened irreparably when her foster brother began to visit her room at night. His threats were cold and unrelenting: "If you tell anyone, you'll be thrown out, and no one will want you." She believed him. Every act of violence against her body became another brick in the wall around her heart, cutting her off from hope, love, and trust.

Over time, the abuse extended beyond one predator. She found herself in homes where vulnerability was a weakness to be exploited. Even when she cried out for help, her accusations were dismissed. "She's just being dramatic," one foster mother had said, her voice laced with indifference.

By the time Tasha aged out of the system, she carried wounds so deep they seemed irreparable. The violation of her body left her wrestling with an overwhelming appetite for love and validation, though it often manifested in self-destructive ways. She hated the cycle she was caught in—searching for intimacy in that only left her more broken.

The Turning Point

One night, after a particularly painful encounter, Tasha collapsed onto her apartment floor, the weight of her shame and regret pressing down on her. The Bible her last foster mother had given her sat untouched on the nightstand. Desperate and hollow, she reached for it, flipping aimlessly through its pages. Her eyes landed on Romans 7:15: *"I do not understand what I do. For what I want to do I do not do, but what I hate I do."*

The words felt like a mirror, reflecting the turmoil inside her. With trembling hands, she fell to her knees uttered a broken prayer. "God, if you're real, help me. I can't do this anymore."

The days that followed were a whirlwind of small but significant steps. She reached out to the elderly woman from the diner, Mrs. Grace, who had written the note. To Tasha's surprise, Mrs. Grace invited her to church. Though hesitant, Tasha agreed. That Sunday, the sermon pierced through her walls of self-loathing. The pastor preached on John 4:14: *"But whoever drinks the water I give them will never thirst. Indeed, the water I give them will become in them a spring of water welling up to eternal life."*

Tasha wept openly, the weight of years of guilt and shame finally beginning to lift.

The Struggle for Freedom

Healing wasn't instantaneous. Tasha wrestled with her past daily, the memories clawing at her resolve. There were nights when temptation whispered to her, urging her to return to old patterns. But with Mrs. Grace's mentorship and counseling at the church, she began to uncover the roots of her pain.

Scriptures became her lifeline. She clung to 2 Corinthians 12:9:
"My grace is sufficient for you, for my power is made perfect in weakness."

When the cravings felt unbearable, she meditated on Isaiah 41:10:
"So do not fear, for I am with you; do not be dismayed, for I am your God. I will strengthen you and help you; I will uphold you with my righteous right hand."

Slowly, she began to reclaim her life.

Redemption and Renewal

One year after stepping into that church, Tasha stood on the platform at a women's retreat, her heart pounding as she shared her story for the first time. "I am living proof that no wound is too deep for God to heal," she told the audience, her voice steady. "I thought I was ruined, but God saw me as redeemed. If He can restore me, He can restore you too."

Today, Tasha's diner shifts have been replaced with ministry work. She now counsels young women who have been abused, helping them find their voices and their worth in Christ. Her greatest joy is seeing others experience the freedom she fought so hard to find.

Her life is a testament to the truth of Joel 2:25: *"I will repay you for the years the locusts have eaten."*

Tasha's story, once marked by darkness, now radiates light. And through her ministry, countless others are discovering that no matter how deep the pain, God's love is deeper still.

That night, Tasha sat in her tiny apartment, rereading the verse repeatedly. For reasons she couldn't explain, she felt a glimmer of hope—like the smallest crack of light breaking through the darkness.

She's In Hiding

***

The following Sunday, Tasha did something she never thought she'd do: she went to church.

She almost turned back when she saw the crowd gathered at the doors, but a familiar face stopped her. It was the elderly woman from the diner.

"Tasha!" the woman called warmly. "I'm so glad you came."

Before she knew it, Tasha was seated in the sanctuary, surrounded by music and voices singing about grace and redemption. The words felt foreign, yet comforting. When the pastor spoke about God's love being unconditional, Tasha's eyes filled with tears. Could it really be true? Could someone like her be loved unconditionally?

***

Tasha kept attending services, though the journey wasn't easy. She wrestled with shame, guilt, and a deep-seated belief that she wasn't worthy of love. But she kept showing up, week after week, clinging to the hope that maybe—just maybe—God could heal her broken heart.

A turning point came when she joined a Bible study group led by a young couple, Marcus and Olivia. Their kindness and patience disarmed her, and their relationship gave her a glimpse of what love and trust could look like.

During one session, Olivia shared Romans 8:38-39: *"For I am convinced that neither death nor life, neither angels nor demons, neither the present nor the future, nor any powers, neither height nor depth, nor anything else in all creation, will be able to separate us from the love of God that is in Christ Jesus our Lord."*

Tasha broke down in tears. For the first time, she allowed herself to believe that God's love was real—and that it was for her, too.

***

Through prayer, counseling, and the support of her new community, Tasha began to heal. She started seeing herself as God saw her: loved, valued, and full of potential.

One evening, during a church service, Tasha felt a stirring in her heart. She realized she wanted to use her pain to help others. With trembling hands, she filled out an application to re-enroll in college, this time to pursue a degree in social work.

"I want to help foster kids," she told Olivia. "I want them to know they're not forgotten."

As she stepped into this new chapter of her life, Tasha's faith became her foundation. The girl who had once felt unworthy now stood tall, ready to make a difference in the lives of others.

Epilogue
Beauty from Ashes

The large conference hall buzzed with anticipation. Women from all walks of life filled the seats, eager to hear the panel discussion on healing and restoration.

At the center of the stage sat Sarah, Emma, and Tasha—three women whose lives had been radically transformed by God's grace.

One by one, they shared their stories. Sarah spoke of rediscovering her voice and using it to fight for others. Emma described how her garden became a symbol of hope and renewal. And Tasha, with a steady voice, shared how God had turned her broken past into a powerful testimony.

The audience hung on every word, many wiping away tears as the women spoke.

"The enemy wanted us to believe we were too broken, too unworthy, too far gone," Emma said, her voice resolute. "But our God is a God of redemption. He takes what the enemy meant for harm and uses it for good."

Sarah added, "If you're here today feeling like your story is over, let me remind you: God is still writing it. Isaiah 61:3 says He gives us *'a crown of beauty instead of ashes.'* He did it for us, and He can do it for you."

She's In Hiding

Tasha closed with a powerful declaration: "Don't let the pain of your past dictate your future. With God, all things are possible. If you can change your mind, you can change your destiny."

The room erupted in applause, but the true impact was felt in the hearts of the women who left the conference that day, ready to begin their own journey of healing.

Final Reflections

It is not just a story of three women—it's a story of hope, redemption, and the transformative power of faith.

To the reader: no matter where you are in your journey, know this—God can take your pain and turn it into purpose. He can take your ashes and create something beautiful. Trust Him, and watch as He turns your darkness into light.

As Ephesians 3:20 reminds us:

"Now to Him who is able to do immeasurably more than all we ask or imagine, according to His power that is at work within us."

Your story is still being written. Let God be the author, and watch as He creates something extraordinary.

Chapter Eleven

An Invitation to Healing

Over the next few days, Tasha returned to Grace's café. She didn't know why, but being there felt safe. Grace never pried, but her kindness was a balm to Tasha's wounded soul. One day, Grace handed her a small, well-worn book.

"This is my favorite Bible," she said. "I marked a few passages that helped me when I was going through a tough time. Maybe they'll speak to you too."

Tasha accepted the Bible hesitantly. She opened it that night in her motel room and read the first highlighted verse: *"Come to me, all you who are weary and burdened, and I will give you rest."* (Matthew 11:28)

Tears streamed down her face. She hadn't prayed in years, but that night, she whispered a broken plea: "God, if You're real, help me. Please."

Chapter Twelve
Steps of Faith

Grace invited Tasha to her church's women's group the following week. Tasha hesitated but agreed, feeling a tug she couldn't explain. The group was small, just six women gathered in the church's cozy fellowship hall. They welcomed Tasha with open arms, sharing their own stories of pain and redemption.

One woman, Emma, caught Tasha's attention. Emma spoke with a quiet strength about overcoming her own abusive past. Her words pierced Tasha's heart:

"Hurt people can help people. When we surrender our pain to God, He doesn't just heal us—He uses us to heal others."

Emma read from Isaiah 61:3: *"To bestow on them a crown of beauty instead of ashes, the oil of joy instead of mourning, and a garment of praise instead of a spirit of despair."*

Tasha clung to those words. For the first time, she wondered if her ashes could become something beautiful.

Final Chapter Thirteen
A Message to the Reader: Let God Take Over

To every woman reading this: You are not alone. Whether your pain stems from sexual abuse, mental abuse, physical abuse, or any other kind of trauma, know this—God sees you. He knows every tear you've cried, every silent scream, and every moment you've felt unworthy or unseen. And He wants to heal you.

It's not time to hide anymore. It's time to come alive.

One of the greatest and most significant lies the enemy tells us is that our pain disqualifies us, is that our wounds are too deep, and our stories too messy for redemption. But the truth is this: your pain does not define you—God's love does. And if you allow Him to take over, He can transform your pain into purpose.

Hurt People Can Help People

There's a phrase often said: "Hurt people hurt people." But I believe it can be rewritten: *"Hurt people can help people."*

Your story, as difficult as it may be, can become the testimony that inspires someone else to find freedom. The scars you carry can be a beacon of hope to someone still struggling in the darkness. When you surrender your brokenness to God, He can use it to bring healing—not just to you, but to others.

The Apostle Paul reminds us in 2 Corinthians 1:3-4: *"Praise be to the God and Father of our Lord Jesus Christ, the Father of compassion and the God of all comfort, who comforts us in all our troubles, so that we can comfort those in any trouble with the comfort we ourselves receive from God."*

Your healing journey is not just for you; it's for the countless others who will be touched by your courage, your faith, and your willingness to step into the light.

Scriptures of Hope Tools of the trade:

When you feel overwhelmed by the weight of your pain, turn to God's Word. Let these scriptures remind you of His love, power, and promises:

1. **Isaiah 41:10**:

   "So do not fear, for I am with you; do not be dismayed, for I am your God. I will strengthen you and help you; I will uphold you with my righteous right hand."

2. **Psalm 34:18**:

   "The Lord is close to the brokenhearted and saves those who are crushed in spirit."

3. **Romans 8:28**:

   "And we know that in all things God works for the good of those who love Him, who have been called according to His purpose."

4. **Jeremiah 30:17**:

   "But I will restore you to health and heal your wounds,' declares the Lord."

5. **Matthew 11:28-30**:

   "Come to me, all you who are weary and burdened, and I will give you rest. Take my yoke upon you and learn from me, for I am gentle and humble in heart, and you will find rest for your souls. For my yoke is easy and my burden is light."

Chapter Eighteen
It's Time to Surrender

Healing begins when you surrender your pain to God. It's not easy, it won't happen overnight, but it starts with a step: inviting Him into your brokenness. When you give Him the pieces of your shattered heart, He doesn't just put them back together—He makes something new and beautiful.

2 Corinthians 5:17 reminds us:

"Therefore, if anyone is in Christ, the new creation has come: The old has gone, the new is here!"

You don't have to carry your burdens alone. God is waiting to take them from you, to replace your sorrow with joy, your fear with faith, and your pain with purpose.

I Speak Life

This is your moment. No matter how deep the wounds, how long the silence, or how heavy the shame, God is calling you to step out of hiding. He's calling you to come alive.

Speak your truth. Seek help. Surround yourself with people who will love and support you. But most importantly, let God lead the way.

Your story is far from over. With God, it's just beginning.

As Ephesians 3:20 declares:

"Now to Him who is able to do immeasurably more than all we ask or imagine, according to His power that is at work within us."

God is ready to do something extraordinary in your life. Will you let Him?

About The Author

Bishop Clarence E.S. Jones, DD – Faith Leader, Community Advocate, and Author

Bishop Clarence E.S. Jones, a native of the Bronx, New York, has spent his life dedicated to spiritual leadership, community development, and the empowerment of individuals through faith. As the Senior Pastor of the Bronx Pentecostal Deliverance Center (BPDC) and the International House of Praise, Bishop Jones has become a cornerstone of his community, inspiring change and fostering growth through innovative projects and transformative initiatives.

Bishop Jones's impact extends far beyond the pulpit. He spearheaded the ambitious redevelopment of the BPDC site at 1755 Watson Avenue in collaboration with Azimuth Development Group. This mixed-use project, known as the "Genesis Project," includes a new 10,420-square-foot worship space, 326 affordable housing units, 16,590 square feet of retail space, and community-focused amenities such as a fitness center and a media room.

In addition to his efforts in urban development, Bishop Jones is the President of the Bronx Deliverance Bible Institute, where he offers courses on spiritual growth and personal development.

Through these initiatives, he equips individuals with the tools they need to lead meaningful, faith-filled lives.

As an author, Bishop Jones brings his rich experiences as a pastor, advocate, and visionary to his writing, weaving together themes of faith, resilience, and community transformation. His work is an extension of his life's mission: to uplift, inspire, and empower others to fulfill their highest potential.

www.ingramcontent.com/pod-product-compliance
Lightning Source LLC
LaVergne TN
LVHW051817080426
835513LV00017B/1989